When you create your life from your spiritual information rather than from your physical desires, you raise your awareness and the awareness of all those with whom you come in contact.

Meditation leads you to your spiritual information, and takes you on a journey of getting to know yourself and your creations.

MEDITATION

Key to
Spiritual Awakening

Mary Ellen Flora

CDM Publications   Everett, WA

You, the spirit, may develop and flourish in conjunction with the proper care of your body and mind. Therefore, the information in this publication is intended to assist you in your spiritual development and to enhance, but not be substituted for, any care you should receive from your licensed healthcare or mental health professional for the treatment of pain or any other symptom or condition.

First Printing 1992

Printed in the United States of America

Library of Congress Catalog Card Number: 91-78135

ISBN 0-9631993-0-7

This book is dedicated to
M. F. "Doc" Slusher,
who has made meditation his way of life.

Table of Contents

List of Illustrations

ACKNOWLEDGEMENTS

I wish to express my gratitude to Bill Broomall for encouraging and assisting in the production of this book.

I also want to thank Sharon Haywood, Alison Eckels and Tom Eckels for editing and proofreading. Their valuable information and support are greatly appreciated.

For the drawings and cover art I thank Jeff Gibson for his creativity and generosity.

In addition I wish to thank Nancy Weymouth for her work on distribution of the book.

Warm appreciation also goes to Lewis Bostwick who introduced me to meditation.

Most of all I wish to express my love and gratitude to M. F. "Doc" Slusher, my husband, who has taught me to be strong enough to follow my path.

MEDITATION

Key to
Spiritual Awakening

INTRODUCTION

For many years I have taught classes focused on spiritual awakening. During that time I have learned that, more than anything else, people need to learn to meditate. All of the answers to our questions are within us. What remains for us to do is to find a way to turn within for our own unique information and our internal path to God. Meditation is the way within to spiritual awakening and the realization that our spiritual guidance is essential for us to create what we need. Because the Creator of all things, or All That Is, or Cosmic Consciousness, or whatever name you use, really has no name, throughout this book I will most often refer to our Divine Source as God.

People have asked me so many times, in so many ways, "How do I find my information to solve my problems?" My reply is always: "Learn to meditate." When you learn to meditate, you begin to remember how to tune in to your spiritual self, and thus, how to tune in to God. All of the answers to your questions can be found within yourself. When you look within, you find the divine spark of God within you. This God

3

Consciousness provides all of the information you seek.

Meditation leads you into yourself as it involves quieting the physical and focusing on the spiritual. Meditation is the only way I know to truly find the answers to your life questions. With meditation, you put your attention back on the spiritual realm within and seek your information there, instead of looking outside yourself for your answers in the physical world around you.

I am sure most people have discovered by now that a new car, a new outfit, a vacation or any other physical acquisition or action will not solve a problem, other than on a superficial level that is not lasting. We also need to realize that our information is found within ourselves and not in the world around us. To solve the major problems or answer the important questions of life, we need our spiritual guidance, which is found within. With only the physical perspective, we continue to create the same problems over and over, because we focus outside and do not listen to the spiritual answers within.

One young man I know has been asking me the same questions for several years and refuses to hear that he needs to meditate to get to know himself. He continues to create disastrous relationships and to fight with the women in his life. He is so focused on things outside of himself that he is nervous, confused and unhappy.

By meditating, he could find the beliefs within himself that keep him caught in this destructive pattern. Through continued meditation, he could clear those old concepts and debilitating patterns.

Fortunately, God sent him a daughter to teach him, as he refuses to help himself.

I hope this book of simple instruction on how to meditate will help many who are asking the same question about how to get back in touch with themselves and their own answers. Many people call me from various parts of the U.S., Canada, Europe and Australia, asking for assistance in their life creations. This book is for those who do not have access to a teacher to help them, as well as for those who want a refresher on the techniques. The simple techniques presented can help anyone who uses them to create a meditative state and receive his or her own spiritual guidance.

There are many examples of people who have used meditation successfully. One young woman called from the east coast, in a state of fear and despair. She was afraid of not being able to live up to the expectations of others. Her fear of needing to please others had become so intense it had engulfed her life. She was unable to enjoy her marriage, job, friends, or herself in any way. The expectations and fear had become a barrier to her spiritual communication, like a veil of darkness in which she felt alone and lost. Meditation was her way out of the darkness of unawareness. By using the techniques, she was able to take back control of her life. At this time, she is learning to like herself as the bright being she is, instead of trying to be what she thought others wanted her to be.

A woman who took a meditation class from a teacher used the techniques to help her clear hate from her body. The intensity of that emotion had created a physical illness in her body. She used meditation to turn within, cleanse herself of the harmful energy and cure the illness.

Whether you have a teacher or use the book to assist you in teaching yourself how to meditate, the results can be the same. You can become aware that you are spirit, with a body through which you create. You are the creator of your reality. Meditation can help you regain conscious control of your creations. You will eventually be able to communicate with your higher spiritual self and your God.

THE ULTIMATE PURPOSE OF MEDITATION IS TO RE-ESTABLISH YOUR ONE-TO-ONE COMMUNICATION WITH GOD. The process takes you on a journey of getting to know yourself and your creations. As you turn within during meditation, you find your path to God right inside yourself. You learn to see yourself as the creator of your reality and the one who decides your own fate. You realize that each lifetime offers learning opportunities and meditation can help you use each life to the fullest. If you do not focus on your spiritual lesson, you will return again and again in other lives until you learn that lesson. Like the young man who refuses to solve his problems and continues to blame others for his creations, you will repeat your mistakes until you stop and listen to your spiritual self and God.

As each individual meditates, communication with God is enhanced for all of humanity. When you create your life from your spiritual information, rather than from your physical desires, you raise your awareness and the awareness of all those with whom you come in contact. Meditation is the process through which we

6

can heal ourselves and our world. It is the path back to our spiritual awareness and our open relationship with God.

My prayer is that all of you who read this simple book will use it to bring the bright light of God into your life. Once this light is within you, it will also bring light to everything around you.

MEDITATION

MEDITATION

Meditation is the cornerstone of spiritual awakening, as it is a time of listening to one's spiritual guidance. Meditation is when you sit quietly and silence the distractions of the physical world in order to hear a message from the spiritual realm. Meditation is a quieting of the mind-body system and an opening of the spiritual system. The purpose of meditation is to communicate with the Cosmic Consciousness or God.

Meditation is not as familiar to most people as prayer. Prayer is most often used to ask for something and to thank God for what we have received. We have all used prayer at some time in our lives, sometimes without being consciously aware of it. We have prayed to have someone we love healed, asked to have our burden of despair lifted, prayed for answers to our questions. Even a wish is a form of prayer, as it asks an unknown source for something; so everyone has prayed in one form or another. Almost everyone has thanked God for something, either out of heartfelt gratitude or from relief.

One problem most people have with prayer is that they are often so busy asking that they forget to listen for the answer. This unwillingness to listen is one reason our prayers often seem to go unanswered. The answers are, in fact, given to us, and we only need to be quiet and listen to hear them. Too often, we behave like children asking "Why? Why?" and not listening to the answer the adult is attempting to give. Meditation is the time of listening. It is the time to hear the answers to our prayers and much more.

Throughout the ages, human beings have sought communication with God for various reasons, ranging from despair over the chaos of the world to the desire to rejoice in the beauty within and around us. A daily communication with God, or meditation time, allows us to have this spiritual interaction. People in most cultures set aside a time of quiet worship during their day. Native Americans traditionally have welcomed the sun and the new day with a morning meditation. Moslems heed their daily call to prayer. Christians have their daily devotionals. Buddhists meditate daily. An investigation into a variety of religions and cultures will reveal that most of them encourage daily meditation in some form. The human race long has recognized this essential need for communication with our Creator.

As we reopen our awareness to the need for this quiet period during our day, we discover that this communication with God is available to us at all times and in any place. We learn that we do not need an intermediary to intercede with God for us, a special place that is more "sacred" than others, or a sacrifice to appease God. We need nothing except ourselves and the ever present Cosmic Consciousness.

In God we are one. We have divided ourselves into bodies to learn and grow. In our division we created religions to help us reunite ourselves with God. The different religions all have basically the same purpose: a system for seeking God. We have gotten lost in the superficial differences and have forgotten the essential truth that we are all united as one in God.

Our meditations allow us to open to the awareness of our individual oneness with God and the oneness of all things in God. Meditation helps us see our ultimate oneness regardless of the path we take.

Since meditation is spiritual communication, it is necessary for us to believe that we are spiritual beings in order for it to be effective. We become more aware of ourselves as spirit as we practice meditation. Just as musicians practice their music or athletes exercise and train for their sport, one must practice meditation to become proficient. The more we meditate, the more capable we become in our spiritual communication. We also become more aware of others as spirit as we become aware of ourselves as spirit. We realize that each of us is not just a body, but a spiritual being residing in a body.

Many people on this planet Earth have forgotten that we are spirit and not just the body. So many ask, "Who am I?" A simple answer is that we are spirit; each of us is a spark of God, manifesting in a physical body to learn how to experience and express God on a new level of awareness. We are in this physical reality to develop spiritually, but we have forgotten why we are here. Because we have become so enamored with our own earthly creativity, we have lost touch with our original purpose. It is necessary for us to learn to meditate to get back in touch with our true selves, our spiritual selves.

We have allowed our ego to become more important to us than spirit. We have engulfed ourselves with limiting beliefs, and have ceased to recognize ourselves as spirit. The more we identify with the limits we have created in the physical world, the more we feel overpowered by them. We begin to doubt our spiritual origin and abilities. We begin to fight this sense of helplessness and loneliness. The more we struggle against our own self-created web of darkness or unawareness, the more we become entwined within it. We forget that we only need to acknowledge our spiritual light and our communication with God. When we communicate as spirit, the darkness of unawareness melts away.

Every person is a spiritual being and is here on this earth to learn unique lessons. Each of us has created our own individual lessons with the guidance of God. Since we have needed to learn so many things, we have created, with God, the experiences of time and space, reincarnation, and other ways to allow a process of growth. God has given us all free will to choose to return to our Creator freely, but we need ways to clear the mistakes we have made which block our return. Reincarnation, the illusion of time and space, and the veil of the physical world are all part of this opportunity to grow spiritually. Through these lessons, the development of our spiritual maturity brings us back to God.

When we complete our lessons here, each one of us is able to become an enlightened being, such as Jesus Christ, Buddha, and the many other great spiritual teachers both known and unknown. We can attune ourselves to God, as they did, by cleansing and clearing the physical barriers we create, such as fear, hate and doubt. By taking charge of the body's desires and using these energies to communicate with God, we begin our return to our Source. By awakening to the reality that we are spirit and clearing away the veil of physical illusion, we can communicate with God as our teachers have. They meditated to experience this communication, and so must we.

All spirit seeks communication, so you will soon come to enjoy the quiet communion meditation brings, if you persevere. Meditation allows your awareness of yourself and all others as spirit, and helps you to see and express your spiritual path on earth. It helps you gain and maintain your spiritual perspective. It assists you to transform your physical reality to your spiritual purpose.

EVERYONE IS A PART OF GOD. God created us from powers beyond our comprehension. We were created to manifest an aspect of God called love. We were given free will in order to make this wonderful manifestation possible. This freedom is necessary, because we must love God above all things and return to God of our own free choice. Meditation brings us the spiritual awareness necessary to master the will of our body and the pull of our physical creations, so that we desire this spiritual unity above all else.

The freedom we have been given has a detrimental aspect as well. With our free will we have nearly destroyed the infinite possibilities of our creative challenge. We have used our freedom to create doubt and to separate ourselves from God, instead of using it to bring ourselves closer to our Creator.

In our creative immaturity, we began to doubt that there was anything beyond ourselves. We doubted the very existence of God. Thus we stopped listening to the guidance from the Cosmic Consciousness. We got more and more lost in our physical world and forgot the spiritual realm. We lost touch with God's purpose for us and created from the desires of the body and the demands of the ego. We used our freedom to create what we thought we wanted, instead of what we were meant to create. We forgot that freedom of will was given to us so we could freely return to God of our own choice.

Meditation is a path back to the level of spiritual awareness that allows us to seek a return to God. When we meditate, we hear what we need to do as spirit. We begin to open ourselves to the spiritual world we have forgotten. By sitting still and listening, we hear the will of God and awaken our desire to return to our Source. We make this journey through the vibration of love that God has created us to manifest.

There are many forms of meditation on this earth. There are meditations to assist the soul to be more in tune with the body and some to assist the soul to be separate from the body. There is no perfect form of meditation; however, there is a meditation which is correct for each individual soul according to its present growth. Planet Earth is a reality filled with dichotomies and a place for us to learn balance. The type of meditation presented in this book is one of balance. It includes an awareness of both spirit and body.

One goal of beneficial meditation is to learn to balance spirit and body. Since the purpose of meditation is to re-establish one's communication with God, we need to be aware that the body is our communication system in the physical world. As we connect the body to the rest of reality, we connect ourselves as spirit through our communication system (the body) to our chosen learning medium (the planet, our larger collective body). When we do this, we learn that we need to clear from our body all foreign and debilitating energies in order to communicate most clearly through it. The clearer the medium, the clearer the message.

This process of cleansing through meditation takes time and space, as do all things in this reality. When we begin cleansing, we discover the energy and information of our parents, siblings, friends, teachers, children, enemies, and all with whom we have interacted during this lifetime. We also discover inappropriate concepts we have brought forward from past lives. Other things we have stored in the body are debilitating energies such as pain, doubt, hate, criticism, judgment, guilt and grief.

This list of cleansing projects may seem insurmountable; however, you do have an entire lifetime to work on healing yourself. Also, all during this journey you will be communicating with God. This enhances your clarity, so your cleansing or healing becomes easier with every passing day of meditation. The important thing is to continue with your meditation and not be discouraged when you discover another project. Like all things in the physical realm, meditation requires time and attention.

These times of communication with God during meditation assist you to pass through the difficult learning experiences of life and to fully enjoy the joyous times. Whether the learning is a creation in present time, the clearing of past experiences, or the cleansing of foreign energies, the quiet time spent in communion with God gives you the strength to continue your pursuit of the Cosmic Consciousness.

Many give up meditation practices after a short time, as they are disappointed by the results. They begin to experience all the negative or painful energies they have created and allowed in their reality, and stop before they work through the difficulties. They expect meditation to bring instant pleasure, immediate peace and enlightenment. They forget that they have been filling their bodies and lives with pain and problems for many years.

Unrealistic expectations block us from experiencing what exists in our reality. When we do accept what we have created, we can change it. We can heal ourselves and create what we want in the present.

When you have broken through the clouds just once, and have experienced the beauty of communication and oneness, the process becomes so meaningful that it is difficult to eliminate from your life. You begin to enjoy your body and your body begins to welcome you. This takes time and patience, and it is well worth the time invested.

The main ingredient to assure continued meditation practices is strength. It is not necessary to be intelligent, talented, good, pure, or anything else. One must simply be strong and determined enough to continue until you reach a level of spiritual awareness that will carry you onward. This means working through the doubt, fear and pain you have stored in your body, so you can fill it with your own spiritual energy. Meditation is similar to physical exercise, as there are highs and lows and plateaus in your progress. When you persevere through the lows and plateaus, you achieve your goals. The debilitating energies mentioned act as a block between you and God, and between you and all others. When you clear them and fill your body with your unique spiritual energy, you open your spiritual communication channels. You experience your oneness with all things.

Since meditation brings a new level of awareness, the process takes time and commitment. Being quiet takes perseverance, and meditation requires being quiet. The spirit needs to re-establish its seniority over the body and relearn how to communicate through its body. The body needs to learn to accept the spirit and to be cleansed of the inappropriate information the spirit has stored within it. This spirit/body relationship is essential to our clear communication. We have to cleanse the ego we have created, which is composed of doubt, pain, fear, hate, and the other misery we have stored in the body. When this is cleared, or even in the process of clearing, our communication opens. We become aware that we are spirit, the body is our creation for learning and communication, and our source and life is God.

MEDITATION

Meditation takes on new meaning when we realize that it is our bridge back to God. It not only helps us raise our own vibration so that we can heal ourselves, it also assists others. By meditating, we raise the vibration of everything within and around us. Whatever exists within the individual also exists in the world. The world is our mutual creation; so when we heal self, we heal everything around us. Our healing ripples out from us and affects those close to us, which affects others, and so on, as it ripples forth through the earth.

We can think of our meditations as a way to cleanse the garbage we have all helped to create, so we can communicate clearly again as spirit. We are like a group of people who have dumped their garbage in the same place in the sea for so long that the garbage has mutated into a living, growing organism. That living garbage then begins to threaten the well-being and even the existence of those people. We have dumped our human garbage of hate, fear and doubt into our "spiritual sea" for so long, we now have our own threat. Some people call this spiritual garbage organism evil or the devil. Whatever name you place on it, the first step away from our earthly garbage dump is meditation. Continued meditation takes you quickly back to the sweet light of God.

Amusement is helpful in meditation, as it lets you move above the heavier emotions of the body. So when you get discouraged by the cleansing project you have created, remember the garbage dump and realize that you can clear it if you simply persist and allow yourself some amusement about your creations. It is easier to clean up a mess when you are amused.

Since most people find it difficult to sit still and focus enough to reach a state of quiet without assistance, there are techniques to help one to attain this space. The meditation techniques that follow can help you experience yourself as spirit and your communication with God. Like anything else in this reality, you have to use meditation for it to work for you. You cannot read about it or think about it and have it affect you, because it is a spiritual process, not an intellectual process. You must sit down and consciously perform the techniques to experience any results. Remember, it took Jesus many years of using such meditative techniques to prepare for his public ministry, so you may want to allow time for your meditations to affect your reality.

Be aware that you may begin to uncover aspects of yourself you do not like, and that this is part of the process. Since all things are permissible in this reality, you may have created many things you no longer want. Simply release what you do not want and strengthen what you like. Let go of self-judgment for the aspects of yourself you do not like. Emphasize the creations that are beneficial and you will reach your goal of spiritual awareness. Be careful not to allow your judgment or expectations to stop you in your awakening. ACCEPT YOURSELF AS YOU ARE, AND YOU WILL BLOSSOM LIKE A FLOWER.

If you get discouraged when your prayers are not immediately answered or your meditations are not instantly bringing you the expected results, remember patience. Also remember that you are unlearning old ways of operating and learning an entirely new system of functioning in this reality. You are relearning the

19

principles of spiritual communication and your oneness with God.

When you are beginning to meditate, it is important to realize that everything is energy. Electricity is a familiar form of energy, normally invisible to us, but visible when it passes through a light bulb. The chair on which you sit is composed of a denser form of energy. It is solid and has mass. Our bodies are made of energy that is less dense than the chair, yet more dense than the electricity. Words and thoughts are also energy. You as spirit are energy as well. You are a very high vibration of energy. You are a much higher vibration of energy than any of the physical reality, including your body.

Through meditation, you can begin to manipulate and use your spiritual energy consciously to create your reality. You will unlearn the concepts that say you are helpless and begin to see your power to create through your physical body. You can become aware of the differences between spirit and body and use them to enhance your reality. You can allow yourself to be the immortal, all-knowing, loving spirit and allow the body to be its mortal, limited self. You, the spirit, are not bound by time and space, while the body is. The body uses effort to achieve its goals, has mass and density, is competitive, and communicates to you and to others with emotions.

You, the bright spark of light which is spirit, are not limited by these aspects of the body. You have chosen to take a body to learn through by using these physical phenomena. You learn by creating through the body. Meditation helps you be more consciously aware of yourself as spirit and of the body as your creative expression. EVERY EXPERIENCE YOU CREATE IS AN OPPORTUNITY TO LEARN A SPIRITUAL LESSON.

When you meditate, you realize that you need to raise the vibration of your body by cleansing debilitating energies from it. Spirit and body are meant to be in harmony and to work together. By communicating with your body during meditation, you can eventually bring the body vibration up to where you can move freely into this reality. You will also be relearning how the body functions and how you can best use its energies for your spiritual purpose.

Through meditation, you can take conscious control of your reality and enhance your communication with all things. Since you are a part of God and God is all things, the enhancement of your spiritual communication through meditation can bring peace and joy into your life.

MEDITATION

MEDITATION TECHNIQUES

Learning to meditate without a teacher physically present to guide you through the exercises creates an opportunity for you to learn to guide yourself. You will find it helpful to have a pencil and paper available to write notes to yourself, or you can use the pages indicated in this book for notes. This will assist in your self-teaching process. You can review the notes you make of your experiences to enhance your use of the techniques and to validate your progress. Use this journal to learn more about the techniques and about you, the spiritual being, and your body. As you write your experiences they become more real to you.

Choose a quiet place. Meditation is an inward focus, so a quiet place will help you achieve this turning within. Meditation is to help you return to the awareness level that everyone and everything is of a spiritual nature. To do this, you must first learn to know yourself. Thus, any spiritual journey is one within the self. You find all of your answers within you. Meditation helps you be quiet and listen, so you can hear yourself and God.

Sit comfortably in a straight-backed chair with your feet flat on the floor and your hands separated and resting in your lap. Keeping your hands and feet apart allows your energy to flow freely.

Sit with your spine as straight as you can. A straight spine allows your energy to flow smoothly and comfortably. Allow time for your body to become comfortable with this posture. It may take you several sessions to feel at ease sitting this way.

Take a few slow, deep breaths to relax your body. Your breathing enhances your meditation and assists your communication with God. Remind yourself throughout the meditation to breathe deeply to relax your body and to release energy to cleanse your system.

Close your eyes and turn your attention inward. When you close your eyes, you tune out the physically visual world and tune in to the spiritual world within you. Whenever you practice a technique, sit back and relax with your eyes closed so you can tune in to you. This posture and the turning within will assist you to achieve a quiet meditation space.

GROUNDING

Grounding is the first technique to use as you start your meditation. Grounding is the creation of an energy cord from your body to the center of the earth. You, the being, create the cord from your first chakra and allow it to flow to the center of the earth.

Be aware of the energy center near the base of your spine, the first chakra. This chakra contains your information about how to relate to this reality. Chakras are simply energy centers that contain information for us to use and master as spirit.

Visualize an energy flow from this chakra, near the base of your spine, to the center of the earth. The energy will flow through all physical matter, the chair, the floor, the earth, until it reaches the center of the planet. Allow the grounding cord to be securely attached at your first chakra and at the center of the earth.

Relax and experience the spiritual connection you have created with this earth. Notice how your body reacts to being

25

grounded. Take a few deep breaths to focus your attention on you and your body. The body may have a different experience than you do. You, the being, may feel joy while the body may feel discomfort. You may be experiencing the joy of spiritual awareness, while the body may be feeling what you have stored in it. Or your body may feel relaxed, peaceful, or safe. Each individual will have a unique experience. Allow yourself to be still and listen to you, so you can get to know yourself and your body.

For an exercise, let go of the grounding cord, allowing it to flow down into the earth and notice what it is like to be ungrounded. Do you feel less safe, less at peace?

Re-establish your grounding by letting the cord flow from your first chakra to the center of the earth. Strengthen the connections at the first chakra and the center of the earth. Take a few deep breaths and relax with your grounding, allowing yourself to experience its effect on you and your body.

Each person experiences reality differently, so allow your own experience. You may feel safer and more solid or you may feel whatever discomfort you have stored in your body. Grounding makes you more aware of your body and your experience in this physical reality. Grounding is the way we, as spirit, connect with the physical world and take charge of our creativity here.

Everyone is spirit, and as spirit, we have created this physical reality to help us learn about ourselves and our creative abilities. The planet Earth is our spiritual schoolhouse: it gives us a place to learn our spiritual lessons. Grounding helps us be connected to and focused on this physical reality, so we can learn our specific lessons. It helps us feel safe in this reality as it puts us in charge. Grounding acts as a foundation on which we can build our spiritual awakening through meditation.

You can be grounded at all times. When you are standing, lying down, sitting, walking or doing anything at all, you can be grounded. The more you practice grounding, the more you will be grounded. Use it in your daily life as well as your meditation time. It will soon become a natural part of your reality and enhance your relationship with this world.

As you sit quietly, experiencing being grounded, be aware of the benefits of grounding. Grounding helps your body to feel safe and more comfortable. It gives the body a sense of security, as it assists you to deal with survival issues about being here on earth. When grounded, you are more in touch with this reality, and so can respond to whatever is happening more easily.

Grounding makes the body safe so that you as spirit can project more of your energy into your body. It acts like an electrical ground, allowing you, the energetic spirit, to flow safely through the less energetic body. Grounding allows you to be more in charge of your reality, as you can create more fully through the body without effort when you are grounded through it. You bring more of your spiritual self into the body when you are grounded. Grounding helps you to be centered as well as connected to this reality. You are more aware of this reality and stronger when connected; thus you are not a "pushover".

For fun, ask a friend to gently push with his or her hand against your shoulder while you are grounded and then again while you are ungrounded. Take a moment to make the transition from being ungrounded to being grounded. Notice the difference in your solidity and stability when you are grounded. This simple exercise can help you acknowledge the effect grounding has on your body.

Grounding has another benefit: you can use it to release energy from your system. You can release any energy down your grounding cord and allow it to be neutralized at the center of the earth. You can release tension, unwanted concepts, foreign energies or anything else down the grounding cord. You can use the grounding cord to release anything from your body or energy system that you do not want, whether it is your creation or something you accepted from someone else.

Experience using this method of releasing energy now. Re-establish your grounding from the first chakra to the center of the earth. Take a few deep breaths and release any tension in your body down the grounding cord. Be quiet for a moment and repeat this release of energy down your grounding. You can release anything this way. You may want to try it, for instance, if you become extremely emotional. You can take a deep breath and release an emotion such as your anger, so you can feel more in control of your body. You can release anything in this way.

You may find if helpful to use your journal to record what you release during your meditation times. You will learn about yourself as you review this cleansing process. Writing these things will help you see patterns in your creativity and will also help you make the spiritual cleansing real to your body.

Visualize your grounding cord flowing from your first chakra to the center of the earth. To practice your grounding, get up and walk around the room. As you walk, be conscious of your grounding. Sit down, unground by letting go of your grounding cord, and then walk around the room again, noticing the difference. Sit in your chair again and reground.

Release any emotion that surfaced for you as you experienced the difference between being grounded and ungrounded. Let the emotion flow down your grounding cord. Your grounding helps you to be in charge of your body and your experiences in your body. It allows you to connect both spirit and body to this reality, and to release anything you no longer want to keep within the body.

Practice grounding every day, both in your quiet meditations and in your daily life, and it will become a part of your way of operating. You can use your grounding to release distractions that interfere with your meditations, so you can be centered and quiet. You can use your grounding at any time and place to be more centered, secure and in charge of your reality, as well as to release any unwanted energy.

Use your grounding to enhance the communication between you, the spiritual being, and your body. Use your grounding to be in control of your experience here on earth. Let your grounding create a safe space for you to meditate and communicate with God. Grounding can help you create a peaceful and joyous experience in this life.

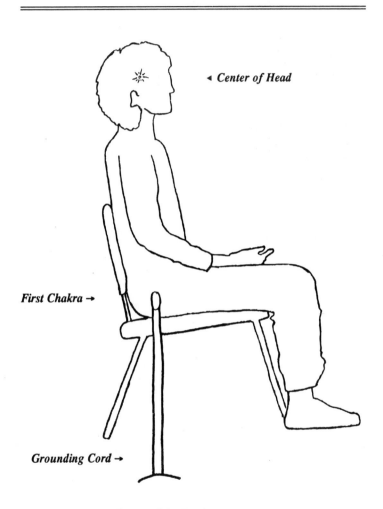

Center of the Earth

Figure 1. Grounding and being in the Center of your Head.

MEDITATION

CENTER OF YOUR HEAD

The next technique to learn is called "the center of your head." You are spirit, and you appear in this reality as a bright spark of light. You have your physical body to create and communicate through in the physical plane. The center of your head is the place where you as spirit reside in the body and are able to remain neutral, without judging yourself or others.

The center of your head is your neutral space, where you can see what *is*, instead of only what you wish were true or only what others wish you to see. This neutral space is where you can abide in the body and see clearly, and be neutral about your creations. Being there is like being in the driver's seat of your car, rather than in the back seat or the trunk. The center of your head is the place where you can be amused and in control of your reality.

Remain seated with hands and feet separated and close your eyes. Ground yourself through the body from the first chakra to the center of the earth. Focus your attention into the center of your head, behind and slightly above the level of your eyes. To help you experience this, place your index fingers, one just above your ear and one on your forehead, between and slightly above your eyes. Imagine a line flowing into your head from the tip of each finger and notice where the lines would intersect. This is physically the center of your head. Take away your fingers and allow yourself as spirit to be in that place.

Focus your attention into the center of your head. As spirit, you go where you put your attention, and as spirit you can be any place instantly. Be in the center of your head. Take a few deep breaths to allow your body to adjust to your presence. It may not be used to you being there so strongly. Take time to experience your attention there and the effect this has on your body. Allow yourself to get a word or two to describe the experience. This will help you make it more real for you and for your body. You may see yourself immediately as a bright light, or it may take you some time to see yourself there. Either way, remember you are a bright light and a part of God.

Notice your grounding when you focus into the center of your head. Allow your grounding to increase to release any tension caused by you being in the center of your head. You are spirit and the body is your creation. You, the spirit, entering the body, can get a reaction from the body. This is when grounding is important to help the body deal with you, because you have so much more energy than the body. As you experience being

34

in the center of your head and grounded, relax and breathe deeply and begin to quiet your thoughts. You can let the busyness of your thoughts flow away down your grounding cord to the center of the earth. You can also release anyone else's thoughts you may have in your head down your grounding cord.

You are the only energy or spiritual being appropriate to be in the center of your head. This area is your control center in the body. Because we love to communicate and share, you may find you have shared the center of your head with someone else. You may discover foreign or inappropriate energies in the center of your head, because you have believed it was the place to communicate with others.

The center of your head is the place from which you control what is happening in your reality. If someone else's energy is there, you will create your reality through their concepts and beliefs rather than through your own. You can release any foreign energy down your grounding cord, and own the center of your head for yourself by being there.

Center and experience this neutral space. Notice anything that is not yours and release it down your grounding. You need to keep this space clear during meditation, as it is part of the system with which you communicate with God.

It is often difficult for us to learn to be separate within our individual bodies, since we are spiritually connected. We long to merge when we are in our bodies, in the same manner that we can when we are not, but we must learn to be centered in our individual body to learn our unique life lessons. If we merge with any other being, we will be learning his or her lessons and we will have to return to learn our own lessons in another life. The center of the head is the neutral, non-judgmental space in which we learn with the greatest control and least confusion.

Many teach that the heart chakra is the place to abide within the body; but if you center there, you will be overwhelmed with its vibration and unable to stay in control of your creativity. When you focus in the center of your head you can have all the vibration of oneness from the heart chakra, without being overwhelmed or confused by it. If you center in the heart chakra you will not learn your unique lessons because you will be experiencing others so strongly.

Being in the center of your head puts you in neutral with yourself and others. It is a safe place for you as spirit to create in and experience this reality. It is the space where you can "be in the earth and not of it". Being in the center of your head, in neutral, allows you to have your amusement about your creations. When you have this neutral view of life you maintain your spiritual perspective and do not allow yourself to be drawn into the darkness of the ego. You begin to see clearly what *is*, rather than what you or others wish to have you see. In other words, you see beyond the facades we have created in this world and you see the spiritual reality.

To help you be more certain about being centered, allow yourself to experience other spaces as spirit. Move your attention above your head and experience the difference. Get a word for being above your head as opposed to being in the center of your head. Move your awareness back to the center of your head.

Now move your attention to other places and then back to the center of your head after every journey. First move to your right index finger and back, then into your left big toe and back to the center of your head. Each time allow time to be aware of how each place feels to you and how your body responds to you being there. Hopefully, the finger and big toe locations will help you experience your amusement as you learn these techniques.

As you have undoubtedly discovered by now, the center of your head is a more effective place from which to run your reality than any other. The view is neutral and not judgmental. The body feels safe with you in charge in the center of your head. The spiritual space located there, contains or allows easy access to all the information you need. The center of your head is where you can focus your energy intensely into this reality, like the sunlight through a magnifying glass, or light reflecting through a crystal.

Breathe deeply, be grounded and focus your attention into the center of your head. Relax there as long as you are comfortable. The more you practice this, the easier it is for you to operate from this space. Increase the time spent there a little each day.

MEDITATION

When you meditate, the center of your head is the place from which you can use your body as a communication system to communicate with God. As you practice meditation, the spiritual system in your head will open and develop. When you put your spiritual attention into the center of your head, you trigger this development. Meditate daily and the center of your head will become a neutral creative space for you.

CORNER OF THE ROOM

We are spirit. We can be any place instantly. The body takes time and space to travel, but spirit is not bound by time and space. We can project ourselves by simply putting our attention where we want to go. We can experience being outside of the body by simply focusing our attention.

Focusing your attention into the center of your head allows you to experience and be in charge of your physical reality and creations. Being in the corner of the room allows you to experience yourself as spirit, separate from the body. Going to the corner of the room is a safe way to journey outside of your body, during meditation.

Since you are not in as much control of your body when you are outside of it, it is recommended you go to the corner only when you are meditating in a safe place.

Be seated with hands and feet separated and close your eyes. Ground yourself through the body from the first chakra to the center of the earth. Focus your attention into the center of your head.

39

Now you are ready to experience leaving your body consciously and safely. First, open your eyes and turn in your chair until you can see the back of the room you are in. Pick out an upper back corner of the room, which will be your destination. Now the body knows where you will be. Face forward once again in your chair, close your eyes, ground and center, take a deep breath.

Float up above your head and then up to the corner of the room. Experience yourself as spirit, outside of your body in the corner of the room. Stay there a moment. Slowly float back down to your body, stopping above your head, and then gently move back down into the center of your head.

Be in the center of your head and experience being surrounded by your body. Take a deep breath and relax your body. Use your grounding to release any tension your body experienced from having you leave it.

You have consciously created an out-of-body experience. When you do this consciously, while remaining grounded, you do it safely. If you are not conscious of leaving the body and are ungrounded, you may frighten your body. Be aware of how your body feels about you leaving it and going to the corner. Notice how your body feels about you being back in the center of your head. You are learning to work with the body, instead of forcing it.

If you communicate with the body as you train it to be used for meditation, you create harmony with it. By communicating with the body you establish affinity and openness with it. You can use your meditations to cleanse the body and learn to communicate with it. As you clear the body of the pain of being forced to comply with your demands and start working harmoniously with it, you create the communication system you seek. When the body is clear, your communication with God is clear.

Going to the corner of the room helps you recognize yourself as spirit separate from your body. You are not your body; you are spirit. As spirit you do not use effort. The body does use effort.

Be seated with hands and feet separated and close your eyes. Ground yourself through the body from the first chakra to the center of the earth. Focus your attention into the center of your head.

Float up above your head and then up to the corner of the room again, experiencing the no-effort flow of you as spirit.

Return to the center of your head and experience being surrounded by the effort energy of your body. You as spirit can be amused by effort when you know you are not your body. You can also allow the body its own way of functioning when you realize you are spirit and not limited by the body.

Try this exercise to help you realize the effect of being in and out of the body: write a column of numbers on a sheet of paper. Ground and go from the center of your head to the corner of the room. Add the numbers while grounded and in the corner of the room. Then come gently back to the top of your head and back into the center of your head.

Count the numbers again after you have grounded and centered. Notice the difference in your ability to do the exercise in and out of your body. Release anything you wish to let go of down your grounding. This exercise can help you realize how being out of your body affects your ability to function in the physical world.

Repeat the technique of going to the corner of the room and returning to the center of your head until you are comfortable with it. Simply moving from the center of your head to the corner of the room and back can help you become more aware of yourself as spirit. Think of words that describe both experiences to help you identify with both realities.

During your meditations, you can be in the center of your head to help you solve problems related to your body. To solve spiritual problems, you can go to the corner of the room and leave the limits of the body behind. Examples of body problems would be finding a place to live or a new job. A spiritual problem would be learning how to change a behavior pattern or how to enhance your communication.

As we learn that we are spirit and have a body to use to communicate in this reality, we also need to learn how to function in both realities. We can awaken to our spiritual selves and learn to focus into the body to learn our unique lessons. Going to the corner of the room can provide us with the space from our physical creations we need to validate our spiritual nature.

Going to the corner of the room is an exercise to be used during your quiet meditations to help you regain your spiritual perspective. It would be confusing to do this exercise in work or play, as you do not have the body control necessary to remain safe during physical activities when you are out of your body. Whenever you meditate, allow time to go to the corner of the room to experience yourself as spirit without the limits of the physical body.

Accept yourself as you are, and you will blossom like a rose.

SPIRITUAL EXPERIENCE

If you have difficulty experiencing one of these techniques, just relax with it for a while. Move on to the next technique rather than getting caught in trying to figure out how to experience the previous one. These are spiritual techniques, and you cannot operate as spirit using effort. Allow your meditations to be a spiritual experience.

Each time you repeat the technique, you will grow in confidence and experience more. It may take a few times using some particular technique for you to physically sense it. Experience is the only way to learn this information, as it is spiritual and not physical.

We have all become focused on the intellectual process of learning, which is an aspect of the physical world. These spiritual techniques require that we move into a higher level of awareness and operate as spirit. This demands a leap of faith in the beginning, as it often takes time for the body to adjust to the new way of being used. The body is comfortable with its intellectual process, but the intellect is limited in its scope, like a computer. When we allow ourselves to expand into our spiritual awareness, we go beyond all physical limits, including the intellect.

As you continue to use the techniques, you will relearn how to operate as spirit with all that is available in your body. The intellect will become a part of this, but no longer an upper limit. Through continued meditation you can become aware of reality beyond the physical realm.

Operate as spirit and your creativity is no longer limited by your body. As you meditate allow the awakening of your spiritual experience.

CREATING & DESTROYING

Our spiritual ability to create and destroy is another ingredient in meditation. We need to be able to destroy to clear away old concepts and make room for new ones. We must create to make the new in our lives. We need to be able to both create and destroy to heal and change. If we create without destroying, we become a slave to our creations; and, of course, we cannot destroy without creating to fill the new space. We need both sides of this dichotomy to balance our creativity.

There are many physical examples of the need to have both ends of this dichotomy. The seasons show us the healing powers of creation and destruction as we watch things change and see each phase play its part in the earth process. As in the seasons, chemical reactions, and all things, when one thing is destroyed, another is created. When wood is destroyed by burning, fire, warmth and ashes are created.

We can see the creative, destructive cycles of earth all around us. In addition to the seasons and chemical changes, there are the life cycles of all living things to show us earth's creative cycles. All living things experience birth, growth and death. Creation is one of God's gifts to us in this reality and meditation can assist us to use this gift consciously and beneficially.

In this exercise, we use the image of a rose, as it represents the opening of the individual soul to God. It is also a symbol of beauty, neutrality and simplicity.

Sit back in your chair, ground from your first chakra to the center of the earth, close your eyes, and be in the center of your head. Take a few deep breaths to help you center and relax.

Create a mental image picture of a rose about six inches out in front of your forehead. Admire your creation. Now, explode the rose. Simply let it disappear. When you do this you free the energy to be reused. Notice how you feel as you do this.

Create another rose and explode it. Be aware that you are clearing your spiritual and physical spaces as you do this. This exercise assists you to create change in your reality. You can release energy down your grounding that may interfere with your ability to either create or destroy the rose.

Create another rose and admire your creation. Reach out with your hand and feel the rose. All creations occupy space and you can feel the rose once you sensitize yourself. Explode the rose and reach out and feel its absence.

48

Create and explode roses for a moment. Simply create a rose and then explode it and repeat this at your own rate. Be grounded and centered as you do this. Allow time to experience this exercise. Allow yourself to experience this spiritual ability and release any expectations you may have. Find a few words to describe this experience to yourself.

Creating and destroying roses helps you release concepts that no longer work for you. This makes it easier for you to get in touch with your own unique information. As you become clearer, you are able to create what is correct for you in the present. For example, you may be afraid of crossing the street, as you are still operating from the information given to you by an adult when you were a child. You can destroy this person's information now, and create your own awareness of how to cross the street. This simple example can be expanded to any aspect of your life.

Focus on your grounding and be in the center of your head. Create a rose in front of you. Get in touch with a belief of yours that keeps you from being creative. Let the belief float into the rose and then destroy the rose. You have just consciously created your reality. You changed your spiritual reality by clearing something you no longer want. You changed your view of this reality by letting go of a limit to your creativity.

Create another rose. Be aware of a belief that blocks you from creating the image of a rose. Release the belief into the rose and explode the rose. You cleared another block to your creativity.

Do the same for anything interfering with your ability to destroy in your reality. Create a rose, release into it a block to your ability to destroy anything you do not want, and explode the rose. You consciously cleared another block to your creativity. We need to destroy in order to create, as these abilities are complementary, like two halves of the same circle; neither is complete without the other.

Create another rose. Be aware of a belief that limits your ability to explode a rose and let it flow into the rose and explode the rose.

Practice creating and exploding roses during your meditations. Each time you do this, you change your energy. You are consciously changing your reality by clearing your space. You can direct your meditations by consciously creating a rose to represent what you wish to clear and exploding the rose.

RUNNING ENERGY

Another technique to assist you in quieting the mind-body system and taking charge as spirit is running your energy. We all run energy already, as all living things have energy and it is in motion. This technique is a way of moving your energies consciously, in a particular pattern to enhance your relationship with both the physical reality and the spiritual realm.

We begin with earth energy, the energy of the planet. It enhances your grounding and assists you to be more aware of this reality and how to operate in it. It also helps your body feel real and safe.

Sit upright in a chair, back straight, feet on the floor and hands separated. Sitting straight will enhance the flow of energy. Close your eyes, ground and center and turn within. Be aware of your feet on the floor.

There are chakras in the arches of your feet. The chakras can be opened and closed like the lens of a camera. Open your feet chakras. Allow earth energy to flow up

51

through these energy centers and to flow through channels that run up through your legs to the first chakra. At the first chakra, allow the energy to flow down your grounding cord. Be centered and grounded and experience this movement of energy through your feet chakras, up your leg channels and down your grounding cord. Be aware of how earth energy affects your grounding.

Allow time to experience the earth energy flowing. Notice how your body reacts to it. From the center of your head notice how you experience this energy. You may find it helpful to take a few deep breaths to assist the energy to flow more freely. Relax and allow it to move through you, up your legs and down your grounding. You may also find it helpful to stand up and move around the room as you run this earth energy, to see that you can use it at all times. Then be seated again and experience the earth energy from this more focused perspective.

Earth energy helps you relate to the earth. Take a deep breath and experience the flow of this energy through the channels in your legs and down the grounding. When you feel "spacey" or out of touch with the physical world, you can ground and run earth energy to bring yourself back to earth and this reality. This energy of the earth assists you to relate more clearly to your physical reality and gives you a sense of oneness with your world.

Take a few deep breaths and experience the flow of earth energy up the channels in your legs and down your grounding cord. Relax with this and allow your body to enjoy this flow of energy. Let the energy be like warm water flowing and melt away any tension in your body.

Earth energy helps us be in touch with how the physical world works. Part of our lesson in any lifetime is how to operate a body and how to function in time and space. Grounding and earth energy help us focus on the body as our creative vessel or door into this reality. When we are focused, we can accomplish our mission here. Think of life as a game. If you know how the game works, what the rules are and concentrate on the game, then you play it well. If you are not focused, do not know or follow the rules, and do not use your body correctly, the game will not work for you. Earth energy helps you stay in touch with the game here on earth.

Our bodies and the planet are ours through which to create. We have to own this reality and attach to it to operate effectively through it. We need to learn how to own and use our bodies, and how to project through them. It is necessary to heal the body and get in harmony with our earthly creations to accomplish our spiritual purpose. Use your earth energy and grounding to assist you to be in touch with your body and your other earthly creations.

Next, we add cosmic energy: the energy of the Cosmos, which is unlimited. Cosmic energy is experienced as vibrations and seen in this reality as colors. We have an infinite variety of cosmic vibrations to use. Use a bright gold energy now, as gold is a neutral vibration. When we consciously bring cosmic energy into our system, we take charge of our spiritual relationship with this reality. The cosmic energy helps us to raise the body's vibration so we can bring more of our spiritual energy into the body. When we focus our attention into the body, we are better able to communicate through it and fulfill our earthly purpose.

Create a ball of gold cosmic energy above your head. This configuration will help make this energy more real to your body. Allow the energy to flow down to the top of your head. Let it flow into your body at the top of your head and flow along channels on each side of your spine, all the way down to the first chakra. Allow the earth energy to blend with the cosmic energy at your first chakra. Then let the blend of energies flow up channels running through your body, till it fountains out the top of your head and flows like a fountain all around your body. Allow more cosmic energy to flow than earth energy as the blend of energies moves up through the body. The system needs the cosmic energy in the upper areas. Allow the excess earth energy to flow down the grounding cord to enhance the grounding.

Let some of the energy branch off at the cleft of your throat and move down channels in your arms and out the chakras in the palms of your hands. The energies in your arms and hands are your creative and healing energies. We use these energies to create on the physical plane. Everything is energy. Energy can be manipulated to create what we want. Let go of the fixation on the body's visual perspective and tune into the spiritual view that everything is energy and is in motion.

Focus in the center of your head, be grounded, and experience this flow of energies: the earth energy moving up the legs and down the grounding; the cosmic energy flowing down the back channels along each side of the spine, mixing with some earth energy in the first chakra, then moving up through channels in the body to fountain out the top of the head and flow all around you. Also allow energy to branch off at the throat and flow out the arms. Allow the energies to melt away any blocks in the channels like warm water melting ice.

Allow time to run your energy. It is a technique that helps you clear your body and spiritualize it for your use. Allow the process to be easy and effortless. If you are experiencing effort, use your grounding to release tension. You can also use a rose to let go of anything that is putting you in effort. Simply create and explode a rose several times to release energy. You can visualize the earth and cosmic energies being like clear water, flowing and cleansing. As a flowing stream cleanses and purifies as it moves, so your earth and cosmic energies act as a cleansing flow through your system.

Because these are spiritual techniques, we have to learn to use them as spirit. This requires letting go of intellectualizing them, and allowing ourselves to simply practice doing them. We need to re-establish our spiritual consciousness in the body, and practicing these techniques helps us do this.

You can release any effort or other body blocks down your grounding. Do it now by taking a deep breath and sending any tension down your grounding cord. Also, create and explode roses to release body tension and to allow you as spirit to be in charge.

Be in the center of your head and experience how it feels to have your energies flowing. Have you felt this before or does it feel new? GET TO KNOW YOURSELF SPIRITUALLY AND PHYSICALLY SO YOU CAN CREATE YOUR REALITY CONSCIOUSLY. By bringing the earth and cosmic energies into and through your system, you balance spirit and body. You experience your earthly reality while maintaining awareness of your spiritual nature. The conscious manipulation of these energies assists you to experience yourself as spirit manifesting in a physical body.

By running our energies, we raise the vibration of our body. This allows us to come more into the body and use it more effectively for our spiritual purposes. Using the technique of running energy to cleanse the system and raise the vibration assists our meditations. Since the purpose of meditation is to communicate with God and our higher selves, the system must be cleansed for this purpose.

Create a quiet time for yourself to run your energy every day. Each time you will create more clarity and thus more open communication. Be in the center of your head, ground, and experience the flow of earth and cosmic energies through your system. Take time to develop your system for communication with God.

As a flowing stream cleanses and purifies as it moves, so your earth and cosmic energies act as a cleansing flow through your system.

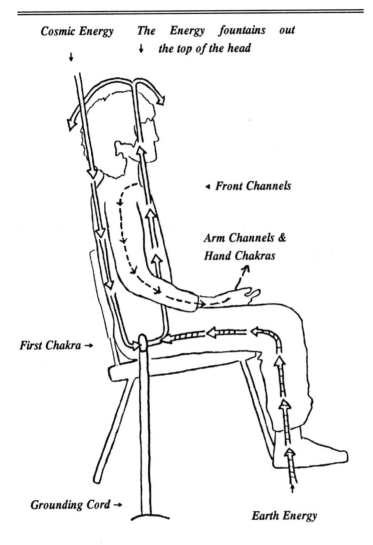

Cosmic Energy   The   Energy   fountains   out
↓   ↓   the top of the head

◄ Front Channels

Arm Channels &
Hand Chakras

First Chakra →

Grounding Cord →

Earth Energy

Center of the Earth

Figure 2. Running Earth and Cosmic Energies.

MEDITATION

THE AURA

Each living thing has an energy field. This energy field is your aura. Your aura indicates your psychic or spiritual space, and is your universe in which you are meant to create. It is the window through which you view the world and through which the world sees you. Your aura changes as you change your energy. The aura is seen in this reality as colors and ideally goes all the way around the body.

Focus your awareness into the center of your head. Establish your grounding. Allow your energies to run. Bring earth energy up through your feet and leg channels and down your grounding. Bring cosmic energy through the top of your head and down the channels on either side of your spine. Mix the earth and cosmic energies at your first chakra and bring them up the front channels and out of the top of your head. Let the energy branch off at the throat and flow down your arms and out your hands.

As your energy flows out the top of your head, let it flow like a fountain all around you. Let the flow of energy clear and cleanse your aura as it manifests all around your body. From the center of your head be aware of your aura, your energy field. Allow it to be over your head, around your torso and under your feet. Let it flow behind you and in front of you, all around you like an egg shell around an egg. Make sure it comes down under your feet so you are engulfed in your own aura. From the center of your head experience the flow of energy through your aura. The aura is in motion and so is the energy flowing through it. Be still in the center of your head and enjoy the flow of energy.

To allow yourself experience and awareness of your aura, expand your aura to encompass the room you are in now. Be aware of how this feels. It may be familiar, as you may be in the habit of doing this to be in touch with or control your environment. If you expand your aura to the size of the room and there are other people in the room, you will be experiencing their realities, as well as your own. You may feel confused or disoriented, or you may feel normal if this is your usual way of relating to the world.

Your aura is like a bubble of energy surrounding you. Because it is your own unique energy, you need to allow it to be close enough around you so that you do not experience other people's realities by engulfing them in your aura.

Now contract your aura until it is close around your body. Experience having it very close. This may also feel uncomfortable, as you are not allowing much personal space. This may remind you of how you feel in an elevator or other close quarters. Notice the feeling, so you can be aware of how you are relating to your aura and can change it when you wish.

Take a few deep breaths and relax your aura to a comfortable distance from your body. You may find that from six to eight inches around your body is comfortable in most circumstances. You can adjust your aura at any time. You can expand it or contract it depending on your circumstances. An example of when many people contract their auras is in a threatening situation. An example of when people often expand their auras to experience others is during a concert or other shared musical performance. People sometimes expand their aura when out of doors enjoying nature.

Be in the center of your head, be grounded and experience your aura flowing around you. Visualize being surrounded by color in motion. Take a deep breath and release any excess energy down your grounding.

We manifest our energy through our space as vibrations, which can be seen as our aura. Everything that has consciousness of life manifests the condition of its being in the form of energy waves. This energy field is our aura. This space is for our spiritual creativity in this physical reality.

Your aura and everything inside it is your spiritual universe in this reality. To fully experience yourself, you need to have your aura around your own body only. When you meditate, pull your aura around you and experience yourself. Your meditations are a time for you to experience your own unique vibration and creativity.

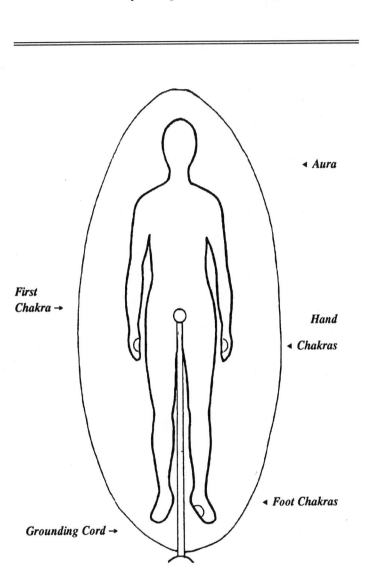

◄ Aura

First
Chakra →

Hand
◄ Chakras

◄ Foot Chakras

Grounding Cord →

Center of the Earth

Figure 3. The Aura.

MEDITATION

GUIDED MEDITATION

The techniques of grounding, focusing in the center of your head, going to the corner of the room, creating and destroying roses, running earth and cosmic energy and controlling your aura all assist you with increasing your spiritual awareness. As you practice the techniques, you will experience more of yourself as spirit. You will be taking seniority over your body and your creations in this physical reality. Have patience and your meditations will bring you new insights into yourself and your creations. Your meditation will eventually bring you to your communication with God.

Your meditations are a time for you to communicate with yourself, your body, and your God. Practice the techniques and allow them to help you to reach a state of peace, where you can experience this level of spiritual communication. As in all things, you will need to practice the techniques for them to work for you. To begin with, a half hour a day is beneficial. You can even divide this into two segments if you need to, until you can meditate comfortably for the full thirty minutes. As you develop your clarity, you may learn to enjoy two thirty minute segments a day. This reality is meant to be enjoyed, so allow your meditations to be a joyous experience.

GROUND. Take a deep breath and relax with your grounding. Allow the grounding cord to flow from your first chakra, near the base of your spine, to the center of the earth. Attach the cord firmly at both the first chakra and the center of the earth. Relax and use your grounding to release any tension in your body.

BE IN THE CENTER OF YOUR HEAD. Use your index fingers to help you locate the physical place in the center of your head. Breathe deeply and allow time to experience being behind your eyes, in the center of your head. Focus your attention there and experience being surrounded by your body. Be focused in this neutral place.

GO TO THE CORNER OF THE ROOM. Look at an upper back corner of the room. Let you, the spiritual being, float above your head and move freely to the corner of the room. Experience being out of your body. Be aware of you separate from your body. Be aware that you are not your body.

COME BACK TO THE CENTER OF YOUR HEAD. Flow smoothly and gently back down to the top of your head and then into the center of your head. Be aware of being surrounded by your body again.

CREATE A ROSE. Admire your creation. Feel where the rose occupies space in front of your forehead.

EXPLODE THE ROSE. Be aware of your ability to create and destroy in order to create your reality.

CREATE AND DESTROY ROSES. Focus in the center of your head, be grounded, and create and destroy roses for a few minutes to clear your space.

RUN YOUR EARTH ENERGY. Open your feet chakras and let the earth energy flow up through these chakras in the arches of your feet. Let the energy flow through the leg channels up your legs to your first chakra and then down your grounding.

RUN YOUR COSMIC ENERGY. Create a ball of bright gold energy above your head and allow it to flow into the top of your head and down channels along each side of your spine. Let the energy flow to the first chakra, mix with some earth energy, and flow up through the channels running through your body. Let the energy fountain out the top of your head and flow all around you. Let some of the energy branch off at the cleft of the throat and flow down the channels in the arms and out the hands.

MEDITATION

RUN YOUR ENERGY. Be grounded and quiet in the center of your head. Allow the earth and cosmic energies to flow through your system cleansing it. For a few minutes, focus on the flow of energies, being in the center of your head, grounding, and creating and destroying roses.

BE AWARE OF YOUR AURA. From the center of your head make sure it is all the way around you, under your feet, over your head, in back and in front of you. Again sit quietly and experience the flow of energies through you and through your aura. Let your energy fountain out of the top of your head and flow all around you.

FOCUS IN THE CENTER OF YOUR HEAD. Enhance your grounding. Experience the flow of energy. Be aware of your desire to communicate with God.

BE STILL AND LISTEN.

ASK AND YOU SHALL RECEIVE

You must ask in order to receive. Information will flow to you from the spiritual realm when you open yourself to it. You then need to listen in order to hear the information. The techniques will help you create a safe, quiet space for this spiritual communion.

The guidance you receive can relate to any aspect of your life. It is helpful to ask about what you need to know and then listen quietly for an answer. In the beginning, you will need to return to the meditation techniques often to keep your system clear and to maintain your focus.

You may find the information you receive unclear to you at first. If you are confused or unfocused, use the techniques to return to a clear, spiritually focused space. You will eventually learn how to translate the spiritual information into your physical reality. Be aware that the information is of a spiritual nature and

71

you may need time to fully comprehend it. For example, the Old Testament contains a symbolic message about destroying our bestial nature and focusing on our spiritual selves. This was misinterpreted and resulted in the sacrificing of animals to God. Be aware of the spiritual interpretation and you will understand the true meaning of your guidance.

You can benefit during your entire life by using spiritual guidance in every aspect of your reality. Meditation can help you receive spiritual guidance on your path for this life. You can ask about the meaning of your work, the solution to a problem or the way to improve a relationship. Any time you become unclear in the communication, or are having difficulty being quiet or hearing an answer, return to the techniques to clear your space. When you have prepared your system with the techniques, simply being quiet and receiving what is given can be the greatest healing of all.

As you take your spiritual awareness into your life, you not only benefit yourself, you also benefit all those around you. You will learn how to be more tolerant, more neutral, and soon will experience the vibration we are here to manifest: love.

As we meditate, we raise our vibration, the vibration of our body, the vibration of all of our creations and even the vibration of the planet. As we solve our own earthly and spiritual problems, we automatically assist others and the planet. When we fill ourselves with light, it shines out all around us.

SUGGESTED QUESTIONS

When you wish to consciously guide your meditations for a particular purpose or goal you can ask specific questions. You may ask any question. You will not receive help if you wish to harm yourself or anyone or anything else. The answers may be clear to you or may take you some time to comprehend. If you have any difficulty, return to the meditation techniques and have faith that they will help you clear your system, so you can have the communication you seek.

When you meditate and are quiet enough to listen, you may want to ask questions similar to these:

What is my spiritual path?

How can I best heal my body?

MEDITATION

On what do I need to put my attention to follow my spiritual path?

How can I improve my relationship with _____? (This can include anything outside yourself such as your spouse, family, friends, job, etc.)

How can I best communicate with God?

What are my reasons for having a body this lifetime?

What blocks are affecting my flow of energy?

How I can best serve God?

How can I best serve humankind?

What is my lesson for today?

Remember you must be quiet and listen to receive the information. You may also need to meditate on the information to know its meaning, as it may take some time for you to interpret its meaning in this reality.

As you meditate and increase your awareness, stay focused on the fact that everything and everyone is a part of God. God is in all things. When we use the techniques to clear the limits we have created and allowed within and around us, we begin to participate in life with greater spiritual awareness. We see that we can all communicate directly with God Consciousness and with any of the great teachers such as Jesus Christ, Buddha, Mohammed or others. Each person has the Divine spark within, waiting to ignite and be a light. When the light shines, the darkness melts away.

We simply need to remember our Divine origin and release the limits of our physical world to return to our original state of grace, which is in awareness of God. Meditation can be our bridge to this awareness. By turning within and becoming quiet, we can emerge into the awareness of light and re-establish both our joy in the earth and our communion with God.

MEDITATION

SEEK AND YOU SHALL FIND

I hope this beginning meditation is helpful to you in seeking your spiritual information and communication. Allow the techniques and your desire to communicate with God to lead you through the difficult parts of the physical maze. Use the techniques any time you find yourself blocked or unclear, and they can help you find your path to God.

Have faith in yourself and your God, and everything else will follow. I have changed my own life with meditation, and I teach others to take charge of their creativity through meditation. Like the young woman who called for help, let yourself find that help within you. Use this beginning meditation to lead you into yourself, where God abides and where all that you need is available. Every journey begins with one step. Take this small step of simple, beginning

77

meditation and follow the path to your spiritual awareness.

Once you step onto the spiritual path, many things will open to you. When you master this simple meditation, other avenues will be open for you if you seek to continue your learning and growth. These simple techniques are a foundation on which you can build your spiritual awareness. You can always use grounding, being in the center of your head and the other techniques to help you focus on yourself and your God, regardless of the spiritual path you choose.

God is always present; we only need to be present also. God is always aware of us; we only need to be aware of God.

God bless you.

NOTES

NOTES

NOTES

NOTES

Rt. Rev. Mary Ellen Flora, spiritual teacher, healer and clairvoyant reader, has been sharing her remarkable insights on spirituality for over fifteen years. She and her husband, Rt. Rev. M. F. "Doc" Slusher, are co-founders and Bishops of the Church of Divine Man/CDM Psychic Institute. CDM is a Washington, Oregon and British Columbia organization based on spiritual freedom and personal growth.

She has taught meditation, healing, clairvoyance and other subjects, and has trained many others to teach them, also. As a teacher, her focus has been on validating each individual's psychic abilities and helping people to recognize their spiritual nature. She is a strong proponent of the use of meditation, and is famous for telling her students to "Turn within and find your own answer."

Mary Ellen's dedication to spiritual freedom and personal growth, as well as her amusement and neutrality, have made her well-known as an inspirational and dynamic speaker. She has lectured and given psychic demonstrations throughout the Pacific Northwest, where she lives.

If you are interested in learning more about meditation, in meditating with a group or learning more about developing your spiritual awareness, contact the Church of Divine Man/CDM Psychic Institute, or one of its Branches, for information on classes and activities.

Church of Divine Man
CDM Psychic Institute
2402 Summit Ave.
Everett, WA 98201
(206) 258-1449

Branch Locations

Bellingham CDM   1311 "I" St.
                        Bellingham, WA 98225
                        (206) 671-4291

Portland CDM   3314 SW First Ave.
                        Portland, OR 97201
                        (503) 228-0740

Seattle CDM   2007 NW 61st St.
                        Seattle, WA 98107
                        (206) 782-3617

Spokane CDM   N 2803 Lincoln
                        Spokane, WA 99205
                        (509) 325-5771

Tacoma CDM   4604 N 38th
                        Tacoma, WA 98407
                        (206) 759-7460

Vancouver BC CDM   P.O. Box 80412
                        Vancouver, B.C. V5H 3X6

CDM Publications *offers...*

☐ ### *The Inner Voice*

A periodic newsletter on spiritual awareness and news of the CDM spiritual community.

A donation is appreciated to cover costs.

☐ ### TAPE:
MEDITATION *Key to Spiritual Awakening*

Meditation techniques on tape. Listen to this guided meditation to enhance your spiritual awareness. Use the tape daily to help you enhance the use of the techniques and open your spiritual communication. $9.95 per one-hour tape.

☐ ### BOOK:
MEDITATION *Key to Spiritual Awakening*

Give the book to a friend or order a copy to use at work during your lunch break. The techniques are timeless and they work when you use them. Put your attention on your spiritual self. $7.95 per book

Prices and availability subject to change without notice.